Olivia Clark

A Little Bit of Magic

A Collection of Poems about Inspiration, Beauty
and Everyday Life

Introduction

Have you ever wondered if magic is just fiction, or if it is hiding in your everyday life? Have you ever noticed that the world around us hides a lot of secrets that might just be magic?

"A Little Bit of Magic" is a collection of poems that will open your eyes to the beauty and magic that hide in our reality. After all, isn't it fascinating to discover how the wind hovering over the trees can enchant us with its noise, or how the city lights at night create a magical landscape? I invite you to discover the magical side of everyday life, to celebrate these beautiful moments and bring a little magic into your life.

List of chapters

Chapter 1

Magic of nature

Amidst the rustling leaves and the soothing breeze,
The magic of nature whispers melodies.
A symphony in green, the forest sings,
As the lush trees sway and their branches swing.

The chirping birds and the buzzing bees,
Add to the enchanting harmony.
A chorus of nature, wild and free,
A symphony in green, for all to see.

The fragrance of the wildflowers bloom,
The fluttering butterflies and the dragonfly's zoom,
A visual feast, nature's art,
A symphony in green, straight to the heart.

In the stillness of the forest floor,
The ferns unfurl and the mosses adore,
A world of wonder, magic galore,
A symphony in green, forevermore.

The ocean's roar, a symphony so grand,
A waltz with the waves, on the soft sand.
A dance of the ocean, the rhythm so sweet,
The melody of nature, a divine treat.

The ocean's embrace, a comforting hug,
The salty breeze, a gentle tug.
The sound of the seagulls, the rhythm of the tide,
A dance of the ocean, a blissful ride.

The sun-kissed waves, a sparkling sight,
A playful dance, in the morning light.
The moonlit waves, a romantic glide,
A dance of the ocean, a lover's guide.

The rhythm of the ocean, so pure and true,
A dance of the elements, a magical view.
The harmony of nature, in perfect cue,
A dance of the ocean, a dream come true.

The magic of the forest, in the dewy dawn,
The light filtered through the leaves, a golden yawn.
The rustling of the leaves, a lullaby so sweet,
The dance of the wind, a graceful feat.

The scent of pine, the earthy fragrance,
The symphony of nature, a joyful cadence.
The chirping of the birds, a melody so clear,
The magic of the forest, for all to hear.

The carpet of moss, a velvety green,
The mushrooms, the ferns, a mystical scene.
The light and shadows, a play of light,
The magic of the forest, a pure delight.

The rustling of the leaves, the whisper of the breeze,
The rustle of the forest, the secrets it keeps.
The magic of the forest, a treasure trove,
A sanctuary of nature, to soothe and rove.

The magic of the rain, a symphony of sound,
A gentle tap, a pitter-patter on the ground.
The drops on the leaves, a shimmering sight,
The magic of the rain, a celestial light.

The scent of the rain, the earthy perfume,
The raindrops on the petals, a crystal bloom.
The rhythm of the rain, a soothing song,
The magic of the rain, a peaceful throng.

The dance of the rain, a joyful prance,
The puddles, the splashes, a playful dance.
The symphony of nature, a rhythmic flow,
The magic of the rain, a natural glow.

The magic of the rain, a cleansing spell,
A new beginning, a tale to tell.
The symphony of nature, in perfect tune,
The magic of the rain, a sweet monsoon.

Chapter 2

Magic of the city

The city of light, a magical place,
A world of wonder, in an urban space.
The neon signs, a dazzling display,
A symphony of color, in the night and day.

The skyline, a majestic sight,
The towering buildings, a magical height.
The streets alive, with a rhythm so true,
The city of light, a dream come true.

The buzz of the traffic, a pulsing beat,
The hum of the people, a symphony so sweet.
The aroma of coffee, the scent of the street,
The city of light, a sensory treat.

The city of light, a place to explore,
The hidden gems, the magic in store.
The vibrant culture, the art on display,
The city of light, a journey to sway.

The rhythm of the city, a beat so strong,
A symphony of sound, all day long.
The honking of horns, the chatter of people,
The rhythm of the city, a constant ripple.

The clanging of metal, the whirring of machines,
The swish of the traffic, a motion so keen.
The buzz of the city, a pulse so alive,
The rhythm of the city, a passion to thrive.

The aroma of food, the sizzle of the grill,
The chime of the bells, the buzz of the till.
The rush of the crowds, a wave of energy,
The rhythm of the city, a symphony of synergy.

The rhythm of the city, a dance of life,
A medley of cultures, a harmonious strife.
The beat of the city, a pulse of passion,
The rhythm of the city, a magic in action.

The magic of the night, a mystical sight,
The city aglow, in a magical light.
The stars above, a canvas so bright,
The magic of the night, a celestial flight.

The streets alive, with a neon beat,
The sounds of the night, a musical treat.
The laughter and chatter, a symphony of joy,
The magic of the night, a playful ploy.

The shadows and lights, a dance so bold,
The secrets and tales, a story untold.
The city at night, a world to explore,
The magic of the night, a treasure to adore.

The reflections in water, a shimmering sight,
The city at night, a canvas so bright.
The magic of the night, a place to dream,
A world of wonder, a heavenly theme.

The soul of the city, a pulse so true,
The lifeblood of the people, a vibrant hue.
The streets alive, with a rhythm so bold,
The soul of the city, a story to unfold.

The grit and the grime, a beauty so raw,
The stories of the people, a world to explore.
The strength and resilience, a power so true,
The soul of the city, a passion to pursue.

The lights and the shadows, a dance so free,
The colors and hues, a symphony to see.
The heart of the city, a place to belong,
The soul of the city, a magical song.

The people and places, a tapestry so rich,
The soul of the city, a world to bewitch.
The spirit of the city, a magic to embrace,
A world of wonder, a treasure to chase.

Chapter 3

Magic of the morning

The morning sun, a golden hue,
The world awakens, to life anew.
The birds begin, their morning song,
The magic of the morning, a rhythm so strong.

The rustle of leaves, the sway of trees,
The whisper of the wind, a symphony of peace.
The scent of flowers, the dew on the grass,
The magic of the morning, a sensory class.

The world in motion, a dance so free,
The magic of the morning, a tapestry to see.
The colors so vibrant, a painting so true,
The magic of the morning, a wonder to pursue.

The magic of the morning, a world so bright,
A symphony of senses, a heavenly sight.
The world awakens, to a brand new day,
The magic of the morning, a treasure to play.

The light of dawn, a shimmering sight,
A world reborn, in a golden light.
The sky ablaze, with a radiant hue,
The magic of the morning, a dream come true.

The world in silence, a peaceful calm,
The magic of the morning, a soothing balm.
The birds begin, their morning call,
The magic of the morning, a melody for all.

The world in stillness, a moment to pause,
The magic of the morning, a moment to cause.
The light of dawn, a time to reflect,
The magic of the morning, a moment to connect.

The world awakens, to a brand new day,
The magic of the morning, a treasure to play.
The light of dawn, a moment so true,
The magic of the morning, a world to pursue.

The world awakens, to a brand new dawn,
The magic of the morning, a world reborn.
The light of day, a shimmering sight,
The magic of the morning, a world so bright.

The rustle of leaves, the sway of trees,
The magic of the morning, a symphony of ease.
The sound of water, a soothing balm,
The magic of the morning, a moment so calm.

The world in motion, a dance so free,
The magic of the morning, a world to see.
The colors so vibrant, a tapestry so true,
The magic of the morning, a world to pursue.

The world awakens, to a brand new day,
The magic of the morning, a treasure to play.
The world reborn, in a magical light,
The magic of the morning, a world so bright.

The promise of a new day, a world so bright,
The magic of the morning, a radiant light.
The world reborn, in a golden hue,
The magic of the morning, a world so true.

The birds begin, their morning song,
The magic of the morning, a melody so strong.
The rustle of leaves, the sway of trees,
The magic of the morning, a symphony of ease.

The world in motion, a dance so free,
The magic of the morning, a world to see.
The colors so vibrant, a tapestry so true,
The magic of the morning, a world to pursue.

The promise of a new day, a brand new start,
The magic of the morning, a world of heart.
The world awakens, to a brand new day,
The magic of the morning, a treasure to play.

Chapter 4

Magic of dusk

As day gives way to night,
And dusk begins to fall,
The sky puts on a show of light,
A spectacle for all.

The sun, in shades of red and gold,
Sinks down beneath the trees,
While clouds, in hues both bright and bold,
Drift lazily with ease.

The world begins to quiet down,
As nature starts to rest,
And creatures of the night come 'round,
Their magic at its best.

The stars begin to twinkle bright,
As darkness starts to creep,
And shadows dance in soft moonlight,
Their secrets they will keep.

The air is filled with mystery,
And whispers in the breeze,
As nature's magic history,
Is woven through the trees.

So let us watch this dance of light,
As twilight takes its hold,
And feel the magic of the night,
As the world begins to unfold.

As the sun begins to set,
And the sky turns shades of red,
The world takes on a different yet,
Enchanting hue instead.

The magic hour has arrived,
And with it comes the night,
The perfect time to feel alive,
And revel in its might.

The colors in the sky are bright,
And the clouds dance in the breeze,
As the world begins to settle in,
And the darkness starts to seize.

The streetlights start to flicker on,
And the city starts to glow,
As the magic of the night comes on,
And the city starts to show.

The stars begin to twinkle high,
And the moon starts to rise,
As the world transforms before our eyes,
Into a place of surprise.

So let us take a moment now,
To watch the magic hour unfold,
And let the world amaze us how,
Its beauty we behold.

As the sun begins to disappear,
And darkness takes its hold,
The world begins to reappear,
In colors of its own.

The sky is filled with deep dark blues,
And purples fill the air,
As the world begins to turn anew,
In the magic of its fare.

The birds start to sing their lullabies,
And the insects start to buzz,
As the creatures of the night arise,
In the world's mysterious fuzz.

The stars begin to twinkle bright,
And the moon starts to shine,
As the world transforms into a sight,
That's mystical and divine.

The city takes on a different hue,
And the lights begin to shine,
As the magic of the dusk comes through,
And the city starts to align.

So let us take a moment now,
To witness the magic of the dusk,
And let the world amaze us how,
It can be so full of lust.

As the sun begins to set,
And the world takes on a different light,
The evening begins to show its set,
And the world begins to ignite.

The colors in the sky are bright,
And the clouds begin to move,
As the world transforms before our sight,
In a way that's smooth and true.

The stars begin to twinkle high,
And the moon begins to rise,
As the world takes on a different vibe,
In the magic of its guise.

The city comes alive at night,
And the streets begin to bustle,
As the people start to take flight,
In the city's nightly hustle.

So let us take a moment now,
To appreciate the evening's spell,
And let the world amaze us how,
It can be full of magic as well.

Chapter 5

Magic of music

Music flows like a river,
A symphony that makes us quiver,
A magic that we can't deny,
It touches our soul, makes us fly.

Notes dance and swirl in the air,
A melody beyond compare,
A rhythm that we can't ignore,
It fills us up, makes us soar.

Strings that sing and drums that beat,
A harmony that's oh so sweet,
A sound that we can't resist,
It moves us all, can't be missed.

Music speaks a language divine,
A magic that transcends time,
It weaves a story with its song,
And takes us where we belong.

So let the music take control,
And guide us to a wondrous goal,
Where we can lose ourselves in sound,
And in its magic, we are found.

Music, oh how it inspires,
A magical spark that never tires,
A rhythm that can light the fire,
And fills our hearts with pure desire.

The notes, they dance and intertwine,
A tapestry of sound divine,
A magic that can make us shine,
And bring us to a higher climb.

From ballads soft to beats that pound,
From strings that sing to horns that sound,
The music lifts us off the ground,
And takes us where we can be found.

It speaks to us in every tone,
A language that we call our own,
A magic that we've always known,
And makes our souls feel less alone.

So let the music fill the air,
And guide us to a place so fair,
Where we can find our muse and share,
In a world of magic, beyond compare.

The music, it can never die,
A magic that will always fly,
A rhythm that can make us try,
And lift us up to reach the sky.

From blues to jazz, from rock to pop,
From beats that never seem to stop,
The music, it can always drop,
And fill us up until we pop.

It speaks to us in every key,
A language that we all can see,
A magic that will set us free,
And bring us to our destiny.

The music, it can move us all,
A rhythm that will never stall,
A magic that will never fall,
And make us feel ten feet tall.

So let the music take control,
And fill us up, make us whole,
Wherever it goes, we will follow,
And dance to the beat, all aglow.

The music, it's inside of us,
A magic that we must discuss,
A rhythm that we can't discuss,
And fills us up without a fuss.

From melodies that make us cry,
To beats that make us want to fly,
The music, it can amplify,
And take us where we want to die.

It speaks to us in every heart,
A language that will never part,
A magic that will never thwart,
And help us find our inner art.

The music, it can never fade,
A rhythm that will always evade,
A magic that will always be made,
And help us find the path we've strayed.

So let the music be your guide,
And take you where you want to hide,
Where you can find the song inside,
And let the magic there abide.

Chapter 6

Magic of dance

The magic of the dance is in the beat,
The rhythm that moves you from your seat,
The music that echoes in your ears,
And wipes away all of your fears.

With every step, you feel the sway,
And your body moves in its own way,
Your heart beats fast, your spirit soars,
As the music takes you to distant shores.

The dance is a language all its own,
A way to express what cannot be shown,
A connection between body and soul,
That makes you feel completely whole.

So let the music guide your feet,
And let your body feel the beat,
For in the magic of the dance,
You'll find a world of sweet romance.

The magic of the dance is in the flow,
The harmony of movement, the ebb and the flow,
The way the bodies move as one,
A symphony of motion, a dance begun.

With every step, a new story unfolds,
A tale of passion, of love that holds,
The dancers together, as they spin and turn,
In a dance that makes your heart burn.

The harmony of movement, a work of art,
A dance that speaks to the very heart,
A language of love, of joy and of pain,
That speaks to the soul again and again.

So let the music move your soul,
And let the dance take control,
For in the harmony of movement,
You'll find a love that is truly meant.

The magic of the dance is in the beat,
The rapture of the music, the sound so sweet,
The way it moves you, body and soul,
And makes you feel completely whole.

With every step, the rhythm takes hold,
And your body moves, graceful and bold,
The beat so powerful, it shakes the ground,
And makes your heart pound.

The rapture of the beat, a dance divine,
A moment in time that's yours and mine,
A passion that cannot be denied,
A dance that takes you on a wild ride.

So let the music fill your heart,
And let the dance do its part,
For in the rapture of the beat,
You'll find a love that is truly sweet.

The magic of the dance is in the movement,
The way the bodies sway, in perfect alignment,
The way the music flows, like a river divine,
And takes you on a journey, through space and time.

With every step, the magic unfolds,
And your body moves, graceful and bold,
The movement so fluid, like a work of art,
And it fills your soul, right from the start.

The magic of the movement, a dance so pure,
A moment in time that's yours to ensure,
A passion that takes you to a different place,
And fills your heart with love and grace.

So let the music guide your way,
And let the dance take you, day by day,
For in the magic of the movement,
You'll find a love that's truly meant.

Chapter 7

Magic of words

Ink on paper, black and white,
Words have power, magic might.
They can lift us to the sky,
Or make us feel like we could die.

With a single word, we can inspire,
Or crush a dream and start a fire.
Words can heal a broken heart,
Or tear us all apart.

In a world of chaos and noise,
Words can be a soothing voice.
They can tell a story, paint a scene,
Or convey the essence of a dream.

The pen is mightier than the sword,
And words can pierce like a sharp chord.
But they can also lift us up,
And fill our hearts with love.

So choose your words with care and grace,
And let them take you to a special place.
For words can be a powerful tool,
And they can make you feel like a fool.

Words flow like a gentle stream,
In a rhythm that feels like a dream.
Poetry is the magic of words,
The music of language that stirs.

With every line, we paint a picture,
A world of colors, a golden fixture.
We dance with words, we sing with rhyme,
And create a space that is divine.

Poetry is the beauty of life,
A symphony that cuts like a knife.
It touches the heart, it feeds the soul,
And takes us to places we've never known.

In the magic of poetry, we find,
A world of wonder, a treasure that shines.
It's a gift that we all possess,
A spark of magic that we should caress.

So let the words flow and let them fly,
And feel the magic that they imply.
For poetry is a language of the heart,
A reflection of life that sets us apart.

In the pages of a book we find,
A world of wonders, a magical kind.
The stories that we read, the words we hear,
Can take us to places that are far and near.

In the enchantment of literature,
We find a path that is so pure.
We walk with characters, we live their lives,
And we see the world through different eyes.

The books we read can change our minds,
And open up a world that we once declined.
They can inspire us, they can make us grow,
And teach us things that we didn't know.

In the pages of a book we find,
The power of the human mind.
For literature is the magic of the word,
The story of life that should be heard.

So read a book, let the pages turn,
And feel the magic of the word that burns.
For literature is a gift to the soul,
A treasure trove that makes us whole.

Language is a dance that we all share,
A symphony that is beyond compare.
It's the music of life, the poetry of sound,
And it's the beauty that is always found.

The words we speak, the sentences we form,
Are the colors of a rainbow that's so warm.
They can lift us up, they can bring us down,
And they can make us smile or frown.

In the dance of language, we find,
A world of wonder that is so kind.
We create with words, we paint with sound,
And we make the world go round and round.

So dance with language, let the words flow,
And feel the magic of the rhythm that you know.
For language is a gift that we all share,
A dance of life that is beyond compare.

Chapter 8

Magic of a smile

A smile can light up a room,
A smile can make flowers bloom,
A smile can bring joy and delight,
A smile can make everything right.

A smile is a little bit of magic,
That can do wonders so tragic,
It can heal a broken heart,
And make a new start.

A smile is infectious,
It spreads like a dream,
It can bring peace and calmness,
To a raging stream.

So let's wear a smile every day,
And keep the magic at bay,
For a smile is the best spell,
That we can ever tell.

A smile is a powerful thing,
It can make your heart sing,
It can light up your world,
And make your troubles unfurled.

A smile can turn a frown,
Upside down,
It can make a stranger feel at ease,
And help them through their unease.

A smile is a little bit of magic,
That can make the world less tragic,
It can break down barriers and walls,
And bring peace to one and all.

So let's share a smile today,
And let the magic come out to play,
For a smile is a gift so rare,
That can bring joy everywhere.

A smile is a thing of beauty,
It can bring happiness and duty,
It can make the darkest day bright,
And make everything seem just right.

A smile can be like a ray of sun,
Shining bright on everyone,
It can warm the coldest heart,
And make a new start.

A smile is a little bit of magic,
That can make the world so fantastic,
It can turn sorrow into cheer,
And make everything so clear.

So let's wear a smile every day,
And chase the darkness away,
For a smile is the greatest treasure,
That can bring us so much pleasure.

A smile is a thing of wonder,
It can make the heart beat stronger,
It can bring light to the darkest night,
And make everything seem so bright.

A smile is a little bit of magic,
That can make the world less tragic,
It can bring us together as one,
And make all our troubles undone.

A smile can break down the walls,
Of hatred and division so tall,
It can bring love and unity,
And make the world a better community.

So let's share a smile today,
And let the magic come out to play,
For a smile is a little bit of grace,
That can bring a smile to any face.

Chapter 9

Magic of friendship

In the depths of life's journey,
A friend can light the way.
With laughter, tears, and joy,
They'll be with you night and day.

In good times and in bad,
They'll lend a listening ear.
Their love and support are yours,
To calm your every fear.

True friendship is a magic thing,
A bond that's pure and true.
It's a light that guides the way,
Through life's trials and through.

A true friend is like a mirror,
Reflecting back the light.
A bond that's forged in kindness,
And never fades from sight.

The magic of connection,
Can be felt in every touch.
It's the hand that holds you up,
When life seems too much.

The power of friendship,
Is an endless source of light.
A bond that's built on trust,
And never fades from sight.

A friend is a precious treasure,
A gift that's truly rare.
With them by your side,
You know that you'll go anywhere.

Their smile is like a beacon,
Guiding you through the dark.
Their laughter lifts you higher,
And fills your heart with spark.

The magic of friendship,
Is the greatest gift of all.
A bond that's strong and true,
And never lets you fall.

A true friend is there for you,
No matter what the cost.
Their love and their support,
Is never, ever lost.

The magic of sharing,
Is what makes a friendship great.
A bond that's built on love,
And lasts through every fate.

Their heart is always open,
Their arms are always wide.
A true friend is a gift,
That makes life's journey bright.

Chapter 10

Magic of love

When love appears, it's like a spell,
A magic potion that we can't dispel.
It takes us in and lifts us high,
Makes us believe we can touch the sky.

With each beat of our heart,
Our soul's longing starts to impart.
And in our eyes, there's a spark,
That we can feel but can't remark.

The magic of love is in the air,
And we can't help but stop and stare.
It's like a dream that we don't want to wake,
A feeling we don't want to forsake.

We are under its enchantment,
A spell that leaves us content.
The magic of love is a wonder,
A mystery that we'll never squander.

Love is a journey, a path we must tread,
A magic that can keep us well-fed.
It's a dance that we must learn,
A flame that we must keep and burn.

Through the highs and lows we go,
Our love remains our one true glow.
It's a bond that can't be broken,
A feeling that can't be awoken.

The magic of keeping love is in the small things,
The little gestures that make our heart sing.
It's in the way we look at each other,
In the moments we share with one another.

We must tend to the flame of our love,
And cherish it like a precious dove.
The magic of keeping love alive,
Is a secret that we must strive to thrive.

Unrequited love, a feeling so pure,
A magic that can make our heart sore.
It's a love that can't be fulfilled,
A feeling that leaves us unskilled.

It's a magic that we can't control,
A feeling that can take its toll.
It's a longing that we can't suppress,
A feeling that leaves us in distress.

The magic of unrequited love is bittersweet,
A feeling that can make our heart skip a beat.
It's a reminder of our own vulnerability,
And of the strength of our own fragility.

We must learn to embrace this magic,
And let it guide us through the tragic.
For it's a feeling that makes us human,
A reminder that we're more than just a mere man.

Love's end is a magic all its own,
A feeling that leaves us alone.
It's a pain that we can't ignore,
A feeling that we can't restore.

It's a magic that we must accept,
A feeling that we can't reject.
It's a memory that we must cherish,
A feeling that we can't perish.

The magic of love's end is in the lessons we learn,
The experiences that make us yearn.
It's a reminder that love is a journey,
And that sometimes it ends in a tragedy.

We must embrace this magic with an open heart,
And let it guide us to a fresh start.
For love's end is not the end of us,
But a beginning of something new and precious.

Chapter 11

Magic of dreams

Dreams are woven like a tapestry,
Threads of life and fantasy.
A world we can create,
Where anything is possible, it's great!

In dreams, we can travel far and wide,
Fly like birds, swim with the tide.
We can be heroes, brave and true,
Or dance with fairies, their magic imbue.

Dreams bring hope and inspiration,
A chance to escape from our daily station.
We can find new paths and goals,
Discover our true selves and souls.

So let us cherish our dreams,
For they are more than they seem.
A realm of endless possibility,
A world of magic and creativity.

In the land of dreams,
Anything can be as it seems.
Fantasy and reality blend,
A world without an end.

In dreams, we can be free,
Fly high like a bird, swim in the sea.
We can travel through time and space,
Discover new worlds, a different place.

The land of dreams is a world of wonder,
A place of joy, where hearts don't sunder.
We can find love and laughter,
Make memories we will treasure after.

So close your eyes and let yourself fall,
Into the world of dreams, one and all.
Where magic and mystery abound,
In a world of beauty that knows no bounds.

When I close my eyes at night,
I am transported to a world of light.
A world where you and I are one,
A place where we can have fun.

In my dreams, I see your face,
And I feel your warm embrace.
We dance together under the stars,
Lost in the magic of love's memoirs.

Dreaming of you brings me joy,
A place where my heart finds buoy.
We can be together, you and me,
In a world where our love runs free.

So let me dream of you each night,
And in the morning, the dream takes flight.
But in my heart, the magic lingers on,
A place where our love can never be gone.

In the night, when the world is still,
My dreams come to me, with their fill.
A world of mystery and wonder,
A place where my heart finds a ponder.

But sometimes, the dreams are dark,
A place where shadows leave their mark.
And so, I made a dreamcatcher,
A tool that keeps the darkness at bay, a catcher.

With feathers and twine, I weaved,
A net to catch the dreams I grieved.
And as I sleep, the dreamcatcher works,
Filtering out the shadows, the jerks.

In the morning, I wake up with a smile,
Knowing that my dreams have been worth the while.
For in my heart, I feel the magic stir,
A place where my dreams and I can cohere.

Chapter 12

Magic of travel

Oh, the magic of travel,
A world so vast to unravel,
A journey to the unknown,
A path that's yours alone.

A step into a new land,
A place you've never planned,
The scents and sights of foreign lands,
A journey that forever stands.

A taste of something new,
A culture that's not your hue,
A world that's far from home,
A place to call your own.

So pack your bags and go,
Let your wanderlust flow,
Let the journey be your guide,
Let magic be your stride.

The world is a grand stage,
And travel is its page,
Where every step is an adventure,
Every path a new culture.

The magic of exploration,
The thrill of a new destination,
The beat of an unknown rhythm,
The joy of a new prism.

The colors of every culture,
The fragrance of every land,
The laughter of every people,
The warmth of every hand.

So let's journey to the unknown,
Let's discover what's not shown,
Let's find magic in the journey,
And cherish memories that we'll carry.

A journey of wonder,
A path of new encounters,
A world that's full of magic,
A world to explore and cherish.

From the high peaks to the deep seas,
From the bustling cities to the peaceful trees,
Every step is a new story,
Every moment a new glory.

The magic of travel is in the air,
In the joy of being somewhere,
In the excitement of exploration,
In the journey's revelation.

So let's journey to new lands,
Let's discover new friends and brands,
Let's find magic in every turn,
And let our wanderlust forever burn.

The unknown is full of magic,
A world that's full of mystic,
A journey that's yet to be taken,
A life that's yet to awaken.

The road less traveled is full of wonder,
A journey that's full of thunder,
A world that's full of new horizons,
A life that's full of new reasons.

Travel is a magical potion,
A journey full of emotion,
A world that's full of enchantment,
A life that's full of empowerment.

So let's journey to the unknown,
Let's discover what's not shown,
Let's find magic in every step,
And let our wanderlust forever be kept.

Chapter 13

Magic of history

In dusty old books and crumbling walls,
The secrets of the past still call.
Whispers of magic and forgotten tales,
Stories of heroes and ancient fails.

The ghosts of the past still roam,
Their tales hidden in every stone.
The magic of history never fades,
Its mysteries waiting to be raised.

The ruins of ancient cities hold,
The stories of heroes brave and bold.
The magic of history we must uncover,
To discover the beauty of one another.

In the pages of history and the books of old,
The legends of time remain untold.
The magic of the past lingers on,
In the stories of kings and queens long gone.

From the pyramids to the castles high,
The legends of time will never die.
Their tales of love, war and glory,
Remind us of our own life's story.

The mysteries of the past we must explore,
To understand what came before.
The magic of history we must embrace,
To discover the beauty of every place.

In the old streets and ancient walls,
The beauty of the past still enthralls.
The magic of history is in the air,
Its wonders waiting for us to share.

From the cathedrals to the ruins old,
The beauty of the past we must behold.
Its secrets and treasures we must uncover,
To cherish and celebrate forever.

The tales of kings and queens long gone,
Remind us of where we all belong.
The magic of history we must embrace,
To discover the beauty of every place.

In the depths of the earth and the sky so blue,
The power of the past is waiting for you.
Its magic and beauty we must explore,
To understand what came before.

From the ancient gods to the heroes brave,
The power of the past we must crave.
Its tales of love, war and glory,
Remind us of our own life's story.

The mysteries of the past we must unravel,
To understand what we can't handle.
The power of history we must embrace,
To discover the beauty of every place.

Chapter 14

Magic of art

Brush strokes on canvas, colors that blend,
A world of wonder, art does send,
With every stroke, the canvas speaks,
Intricacies, in every form it leaks.

From paintings, sculptures, music and more,
The beauty of art, you can't ignore,
For in its soul lies a magic so rare,
The ability to enchant, it does share.

A canvas filled with hues and light,
A sculpture crafted to delight,
A melody that touches the heart,
Art, in its essence, is an enchanted art.

For when you gaze at a piece so divine,
You get lost in it, like in a dream so fine,
It weaves a spell, takes you far away,
And in its beauty, you find your way.

With a stroke of a pen or a brush so fine,
Creation takes place, magic divine,
In the mind's eye, it all begins,
A world of enchantment, it brings within.

From the ink that flows on the page,
To the colors that dance on a stage,
Creation takes flight, a dream come true,
A world of magic, it unveils anew.

For in its essence, creation holds,
A power so great, a story that's told,
A tale of wonder, an adventure in store,
Enchantment that lasts forevermore.

For when you create, a part of you,
Lives on in your art, so pure and true,
A piece of your soul, that you impart,
In every creation, a little bit of your heart.

With every stroke, the brush does glide,
On the canvas, it creates a tide,
Of colors so vivid, a story it weaves,
A world of enchantment, it achieves.

The brush dances, like a ballerina so fine,
Creating magic, with every line,
Intricacies, in every form it takes,
A masterpiece, it creates.

For in its touch lies a magic so rare,
An ability to enchant, it does share,
With every stroke, a world does appear,
A place of wonder, that's always near.

So, let the brush, create its spell,
In every creation, let it dwell,
For in its essence, lies a power so great,
A world of enchantment, it does create.

With every stroke, expression takes hold,
A world of emotion, it does unfold,
Through colors, lines, and form,
A world of enchantment, it does transform.

From the dark hues of melancholy,
To the vibrant shades of pure ecstasy,
Expression takes flight, a journey so true,
A world of magic, it unveils anew.

For in its essence, expression does hold,
A power so great, a story that's told,
A tale of wonder, an adventure in store,
Enchantment that lasts forevermore.

Chapter 15

Magic of silence

In the stillness of the night,
When the world is dark and quiet,
The magic of silence comes to life,
Bringing forth a sense of delight.

As I sit in the silence,
I feel my thoughts unwind,
My mind is clear, my heart is light,
And my soul is deeply aligned.

In this moment of pure serenity,
I discover a new sense of peace,
A feeling that fills me with energy,
And makes all my worries cease.

The magic of silence is a gift,
A precious treasure to behold,
For it brings me back to myself,
And helps me feel whole.

So I embrace this silence within,
And let it fill me with grace,
For it is in the stillness of the moment,
That I find my sacred space.

In the quiet of the morning,
When the world is just awakening,
I hear the language of silence,
And it speaks to me without saying.

The rustle of leaves, the chirping of birds,
The gentle hum of the breeze,
All of these sounds are part of a chorus,
That whispers secrets to me with ease.

For the magic of silence is not just about,
The absence of sound or noise,
It is about the way that nature speaks,
And how it brings us inner poise.

In this world that is so noisy and fast,
We forget to listen and hear,
The messages that silence conveys,
And the wisdom that it holds dear.

So let us embrace the language of silence,
And let it guide us on our way,
For in its hush and stillness,
We can find our truest day.

In the depth of the forest,
Where the trees are tall and grand,
There lies a magic in the silence,
That is more than we can understand.

For in this quiet and peaceful place,
We can feel the power of nature's grace,
As it surrounds us with its beauty,
And fills our hearts with its embrace.

The rustling of leaves, the chirping of birds,
The sound of a distant stream,
All of these things are part of the magic,
That makes the silence seem like a dream.

But this dream is real, and it holds within,
A power that we can't deny,
For in the stillness of the moment,
We can find a strength that will never die.

So let us take a moment to be still,
And feel the magic of the silence,
For it is in this place of inner peace,
That we can find our highest guidance.

In the silence of the evening,
When the day has come to rest,
There is a magic in the stillness,
That is simply the very best.

For in this moment of sweet surrender,
We can feel the rhythm of the night,
As it carries us on its wings,
And fills us with its gentle light.

The rustle of leaves, the chirping of crickets,
The sound of a distant owl,
All of these things are part of the dance,
That makes the silence seem like a howl.

But this howl is one of joy and beauty,
For it is the music of the night,
A symphony of sounds and silence,
That fills our hearts with its might.

So let us dance in the silence,
And let it guide us on our way,
For in the stillness of the moment,
We can find a love that will forever stay.

Chapter 16

Magic of colors

The world is full of colors,
A rainbow of hues and shades,
Each one holding its own magic,
A mystery waiting to be unveiled.

From the blue of the sky above,
To the green of the grass below,
Each color tells a story,
And lets its magic show.

The red of a rose in bloom,
The orange of a fiery sunset,
These colors evoke emotions,
That we can never forget.

For the magic of colors is not just,
In the way that they look or seem,
It is in the way they touch our hearts,
And fill our souls with gleam.

So let us celebrate the colors of life,
And the magic that they bring,
For they are a reminder of the beauty,
That makes our hearts sing.

In the world of colors so bright,
There is a mystery in black and white,
For these shades are not colors at all,
Yet they hold a power that never falls.

Black is the color of mystery and depth,
A shadowy hue that fills us with respect,
While white is the color of purity and light,
A shining beacon that guides us through the night.

Together, black and white create a dance,
A yin and yang that enchants,
For they hold within their duality,
A magic that is pure and free.

So let us explore the mystery of black and white,
And the magic that they hold,
For they are a reminder of the balance,
That makes our world whole.

In the sky above, there lies a wonder,
A rainbow of colors that stretch and thunder,
From red to violet, they form a bridge,
That fills our hearts with a magical image.

Each color of the rainbow holds its own power,
A magic that we cannot devour,
From the passion of red to the calm of blue,
Each hue is a story that is true.

For the magic of the rainbow is not just,
In the way that it looks or seems,
It is in the way it fills our hearts,
And makes our spirits gleam.

So let us celebrate the magic of the rainbow,
And the beauty that it brings,
For it is a reminder of the joy,
That colors can surely sing.

In the world of colors, there is one,
That stands above the rest,
A color that holds a magic,
That is truly the very best.

It is the color of love,
A shade of red that shines so bright,
It fills our hearts with passion,
And guides us through the night.

For love is a magic all its own,
A color that can never fade,
It fills our world with beauty,
And never leaves us dismayed.

So let us celebrate the colors of love,
And the magic that they bring,
For they are a reminder of the power,
That makes our hearts sing.

Chapter 17

Magic of food

There is a magic in the food we eat,
A taste that fills us with delight,
From savory to sweet, each bite a treat,
A symphony that enchants our sight.

For food is more than just sustenance,
It is a wonder that fills our soul,
With flavors that evoke memories,
And stories that have yet to be told.

A hint of salt, a dash of spice,
The magic of taste is so nice,
It fills our senses with pure delight,
And makes our hearts take flight.

So let us savor each bite we eat,
And celebrate the magic of taste,
For it is a reminder of the joy,
That food can surely create.

There is a magic in the air we breathe,
A scent that fills us with delight,
From earthy to floral, each one a dream,
An enchantment that evokes pure sight.

For food is more than just a flavor,
It is a fragrance that fills our soul,
With memories of days gone by,
And dreams that we hope to behold.

A whiff of cinnamon, a hint of rose,
The magic of aroma never grows old,
It fills our senses with pure delight,
And makes our hearts take flight.

So let us cherish each scent we smell,
And celebrate the magic of aroma,
For it is a reminder of the joy,
That food can bring with its aroma.

There is a magic in the food we touch,
A texture that fills us with delight,
From crispy to creamy, each bite a clutch,
A spell that enchants our sight.

For food is more than just a taste,
It is a texture that fills our soul,
With sensations that evoke feelings,
And emotions that make us whole.

A crunch of potato chips, a smoothness of cream,
The magic of texture is like a dream,
It fills our senses with pure delight,
And makes our hearts take flight.

So let us appreciate each texture we feel,
And celebrate the magic of texture,
For it is a reminder of the joy,
That food can bring with its texture.

There is a magic in the food we share,
A community that fills us with delight,
From potlucks to picnics, each meal a flare,
A bond that enchants our sight.

For food is more than just a flavor,
Aroma, or texture to behold,
It is a shared experience,
That brings us closer as we grow old.

A laugh over a bowl of soup, a smile over a slice of pie,
The magic of sharing is a reason to try,
It fills our senses with pure delight,
And makes our hearts take flight.

So let us cherish each meal we share,
And celebrate the magic of sharing,
For it is a reminder of the joy,
That food can bring with its sharing.

Chapter 18

Magic of animals

The magic of animals is all around,
From the tiniest bug to the largest hound,
Each one a wonder to behold,
With stories and secrets left untold.

The flutter of wings, the roar of the lion,
The magic of wildlife is truly inspiring,
It fills our hearts with pure delight,
And awakens our senses to new heights.

For animals are more than just creatures,
They are companions and friends to treasure,
With their own personalities and quirks,
And lessons to teach us that truly work.

So let us honor the beauty of wildlife,
And celebrate the magic of their lives,
For they remind us of the joy,
That comes with a simple, animalistic vibe.

The magic of animals is in their pack,
From wolves to elephants, they have each other's back,
A bond that is both strong and true,
A family that knows what to do.

For animals are more than just individuals,
They are members of a team, a pack of equals,
With each one bringing their own unique skill,
To create a bond that nothing can kill.

So let us cherish the pack and its power,
And celebrate the magic of its hour,
For it is a reminder of the joy,
That comes with a pack that is greater than just you and I.

The magic of animals is in their love,
From cats to dogs, they show it like a dove,
A bond that is both loyal and true,
A friendship that can see us through.

For animals are more than just companions,
They are family members, loyal without conditions,
With each one bringing their own unique personality,
To create a bond that is truly lovely.

A purr in the night, a wagging tail,
The magic of a pet can never fail,
It fills our hearts with pure delight,
And makes our souls take flight.

So let us honor the love of our pets,
And celebrate the magic of their sets,
For they remind us of the joy,
That comes with a furry, four-legged friend, oh boy!

The magic of animals is in their world,
From the forest to the ocean, they unfurl,
A majesty that is both wild and true,
A wonder that is a part of me and you.

For animals are more than just creatures,
They are a part of nature's unique features,
With each one playing a vital role,
In the circle of life, that keeps our planet whole.

A flock of birds, a pod of whales,
The magic of nature never fails,
It fills our hearts with pure delight,
And reminds us of the beauty in our sight.

So let us cherish the majesty of nature,
And celebrate the magic of its nurture,
For it is a reminder of the joy,
That comes with living in harmony,
With the animal kingdom and its ploy.

Chapter 19

Magic of the moment

In moments small and fleeting,
The magic of life's fleeting,
Each moment a precious treasure,
A memory to hold forever.

A smile from a stranger,
A breeze that whispers danger,
The moments that we often miss,
The little things that bring us bliss.

A laugh shared with a friend,
A sunset that seems to never end,
The magic of a moment caught,
A treasure that can't be bought.

In moments both big and small,
The magic of life is found in all,
So cherish each and every day,
And hold those memories close in every way.

The rhythm of life is like a dance,
A never-ending flow of circumstance,
The magic of the moment in every step,
A precious memory we'll always kept.

The music of life plays on and on,
With each step taken, a new song is born,
The dance of time, a constant motion,
A beautiful art, with endless emotion.

As we move through time, our steps may change,
But the magic of the moment remains the same,
A dance of life, forever moving,
A never-ending rhythm, forever grooving.

So dance along to life's sweet tune,
Embrace the magic that lies in every move,
For life is a dance, a magical art,
A beautiful rhythm that flows through every heart.

In the moment, there is magic,
A beauty that is truly tragic,
For the moment quickly passes by,
And we're left to wonder why.

The beauty of now is fleeting,
A moment that's always worth repeating,
For in the moment, we truly see,
The beauty of life's grand mystery.

So pause for a moment, take it all in,
Let the magic of the moment begin,
For in the beauty of now, we find,
The joy and wonder that's left behind.

In every moment, there is wonder,
A beauty that we often squander,
But in the magic of the present,
A world of wonder is truly evident.

A bird that soars high above,
A flower that blooms in a garden of love,
The beauty of the world around,
Is truly a treasure that's always found.

In the magic of the moment, we discover,
A world of wonder, waiting to uncover,
The beauty of life, both big and small,
A precious gift, given to us all.

Chapter 20

Magic of life

Life is a wonder, a mystery untold,
A journey of ups and downs, stories unfold.
Every breath we take, every step we make,
Is a miracle of life, a chance to create.

From the first cry of a newborn child,
To the last breath of an elder so mild,
Life is a tapestry, woven with love,
A magic so potent, it shines above.

The sunrise brings hope, a brand new day,
The sunset a promise, that all will be okay.
The stars above twinkle, like diamonds so bright,
A reminder that magic is always in sight.

The laughter of children, the smile of a friend,
The love of a family, that never will end.
These are the things, that make life so sweet,
A reminder that magic is everywhere we meet.

Life is a spell, a wondrous surprise,
A journey of magic, that we can't deny.
Every moment we live, every breath we take,
Is a chance to discover, what magic can make.

From the blooming of flowers, to the song of a bird,
The whisper of leaves, the rustle of herd,
Life is a dance, a rhythm divine,
A magic so potent, it's almost a sign.

The rain that falls, the sun that shines,
The wind that blows, the moon that chimes,
These are the things, that make life so grand,
A reminder that magic is close at hand.

The touch of a lover, the embrace of a friend,
The warmth of a hearth, that will never end,
These are the moments, that make life so sweet,
A reminder that magic is always at our feet.

Life is a marvel, a mystery to behold,
A journey of wonder, stories untold.
Every beat of our heart, every step we take,
Is a chance to explore, what magic can make.

From the flight of a bird, to the roar of the sea,
The rustle of leaves, the hum of a bee,
Life is a symphony, a tune so divine,
A magic so potent, it's hard to define.

The sun that rises, the moon that sets,
The stars that twinkle, the dew that wets,
These are the things, that make life so dear,
A reminder that magic is always near.

The touch of a hand, the kiss of a lover,
The hug of a friend, that will never be over,
These are the moments, that make life complete,
A reminder that magic is always at our feet.

Life is a delight, a treasure so rare,
A journey of joy, that we should all share.
Every breath we take, every smile we make,
Is a chance to savor, what magic can create.

From the flutter of a butterfly, to the roar of a lion,
The buzz of a bee, the purr of a kitten,
Life is a feast, a banquet divine,
A magic so potent, it's almost a shrine.

The snow that falls, the rain that pours,
The breeze that blows, the ocean that roars,
These are the things, that make life so grand,
A reminder that magic is close at hand.

The laughter of children, the love of a pet,
The warmth of a home, that we'll never forget,
These are the moments, that make life so sweet,
A reminder that magic is always at our feet.

Enter the world of Jitters & Glitters, a five-book series that will take you on a poetic journey through the magic of everyday life. Explore the beauty hidden in reality through enchanting poems that evoke powerful emotions and take you on unforgettable adventures. Engage your senses with evocative literature that prompts reflection on life's mysteries and secrets. Immerse yourself in the enchantment of nature and cityscapes, and experience the perception-altering power of imagination. Whether it's love, nostalgia, or the power of nature that you seek, Jitters & Glitters has it all. Let our poems take you on a sensory journey, and discover the intensity of poetic perception and the art of creative expression. Celebrate the fascinating moments that bring wonder and joy, and bring a little magic into your life through inspiring poetry.

Printed in Great Britain
by Amazon

27468322R00076